# LET'S EXPLORE THE STATES

# Mid-Atlantic

## Delaware
## District of Columbia
## Maryland

*LeeAnne Gelletly*

**Mason Crest**
450 Parkway Drive, Suite D
Broomall, PA 19008
www.masoncrest.com

Printed and bound in the United States of America.

CPSIA Compliance Information: Batch #LES2015.
For further information, contact Mason Crest at 1-866-MCP-Book.

First printing
1 3 5 7 9 8 6 4 2

Library of Congress Cataloging-in-Publication Data

Gelletly, LeeAnne.
  The Mid-Atlantic states : Delaware, Maryland, and Washington, D.C. / LeeAnne Gelletly.
      pages cm. — (Let's explore the states)
  Includes bibliographical references and index.
  ISBN 978-1-4222-3327-6 (hc)
  ISBN 978-1-4222-8612-8 (ebook)
  1. Atlantic States—Juvenile literature.  2. Delaware—Juvenile literature.
  3. Maryland—Juvenile literature.  4. Washington (D.C.)—Juvenile literature.  I. Title.
  F106.G44 2015
  975—dc23
                               2014050197

Let's Explore the States series ISBN: 978-1-4222-3319-1

**About the Author:** LeeAnne Gelletly is the author of several biographies, including books on Harriet Beecher Stowe, Mae Jemison, Roald Dahl, Ida Tarbell, and John Marshall.

**Picture Credits:** Action Sports Photography: 22 (bottom left); Delaware Government Information Center, 21 (bottom), 23; Independence National Historical Park, Philadelphia, 30; Library of Congress: 14, 15, 31, 32, 35, 36, 51, 53, 54 (right); Lone Wolf Photos: 49; National Park Service: 29, 33, 34, 54 (left), 55; used under license from Shutterstock, Inc.: 5 (bottom), 6, 10, 26, 46, 48; Jon Bilous / Shutterstock.com: 19, 61; Stephen Bonk / Shutterstock.com: 20; S. Borisov/Shutterstock.com: 52; Orhan Cam/Shutterstock.com: 1, 43; Maria Egupova/Shutterstock.com: 47; Melissa Fague/Shutterstock.com: 9; Brandon Hirt/Shutterstock.com: 16; Glynnis Jones/Shutterstock.com: 57; Lissandra Melo: Shutterstock: 5 (top), 41; Dave Newman/Shutterstock.com: 18; Heath Oldham/Shutterstock.com: 59; A. Paterson / Shutterstock.com: 50; Ryan Rodrick Beiler/Shutterstock.com: 38, 39; Daniel M. Silva/Shutterstock.com: 12; Jerry Zitterman / Shutterstock.com: 22 (bottom right); Mehgan Murphy, Smithsonian's National Zoo: 44; Spirit of America: 11; U.S. Air Force photo / Jason Minto: 17; U.S. Navy photo/Chad Runge: 56; University of Delaware, 22 (top); White House photo: 21 (top).

# Table of Contents

**KEY ICONS TO LOOK FOR:**

**Words to Understand:** These words with their easy-to-understand definitions will increase the reader's understanding of the text, while building vocabulary skills.

**Sidebars:** This boxed material within the main text allows readers to build knowledge, gain insights, explore possibilities, and broaden their perspectives by weaving together additional information to provide realistic and holistic perspectives.

**Research Projects:** Readers are pointed toward areas of further inquiry connected to each chapter. Suggestions are provided for projects that encourage deeper research and analysis.

**Text-Dependent Questions:** These questions send the reader back to the text for more careful attention to the evidence presented there.

**Series Glossary of Key Terms:** This back-of-the book glossary contains terminology used throughout this series. Words found here increase the reader's ability to read and comprehend higher-level books and articles in this field.

# LET'S EXPLORE THE STATES

**Atlantic:** North Carolina, Virginia, West Virginia
**Central Mississippi River Basin:** Arkansas, Iowa, Missouri
**East South-Central States:** Kentucky, Tennessee
**Eastern Great Lakes:** Indiana, Michigan, Ohio
**Gulf States:** Alabama, Louisiana, Mississippi
**Lower Atlantic:** Florida, Georgia, South Carolina
**Lower Plains:** Kansas, Nebraska
**Mid-Atlantic:** Delaware, District of Columbia, Maryland
**Non-Continental:** Alaska, Hawaii
**Northern New England:** Maine, New Hampshire, Vermont
**Northeast:** New Jersey, New York, Pennsylvania
**Northwest:** Idaho, Oregon, Washington
**Rocky Mountain:** Colorado, Utah, Wyoming
**Southern New England:** Connecticut, Massachusetts, Rhode Island
**Southwest:** New Mexico, Oklahoma, Texas
**U.S. Territories and Possessions**
**Upper Plains:** Montana, North Dakota, South Dakota
**The West:** Arizona, California, Nevada
**Western Great Lakes:** Illinois, Minnesota, Wisconsin

DECEMBER 7, 1787

 **Delaware at a Glance**

**Area:** 2,489 sq miles (6,447 sq km). 49th-largest state[1]
  *Land:* 1,949 sq mi (5,048 sq km)
  *Water:* 540 sq mi (1,399 sq km)
**Highest elevation:** Ebright Azimuth benchmark monument in New Castle County, 448 feet (137 m)
**Lowest elevation:** Atlantic Ocean (sea level)

**Statehood:** Dec. 7, 1787 (1st state)
**Capital:** Dover

**Population:** 935,614 (45th largest state)[2]

**State nickname:** The First State, Diamond State, Small Wonder
**State bird:** Blue Hen chicken
**State flower:** peach blossom

[1] *U.S. Census Bureau*
[2] *U.S. Census Bureau, 2014 estimate*

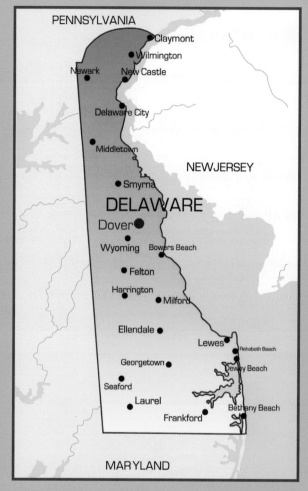

# Delaware

The residents of Delaware, known as Delawareans, proclaim on their car license plates that they live in "the First State." The nickname does not refer to size—Delaware is actually is the second smallest state in the nation. (Only Rhode Island is smaller.) Instead, the nickname reflects Delaware's history. The state was the first of the original 13 colonies to join the United States of America. Delaware *ratified* the U.S. *Constitution* on December 7, 1787. Delawareans sometimes call their land the state that started a nation.

## Geography

Delaware is just 96 miles (155 kilometers) long and varies between 9 and 35 miles (15 and 56 km) wide. It is bordered by Pennsylvania to the north and Maryland to the west and south. New Jersey, the Delaware Bay, Delaware River, and Atlantic Ocean lie to the east.

The First State is part of the *Delmarva Peninsula*, so named because it includes lands from DELaware, MARyland, and VirginiA. Delaware is the only state in the nation with a circular boundary. A small arc separates Delaware from Pennsylvania.

This boundary line was originally created as a 12-mile (19 km) measurement from the courthouse in the city of New Castle.

Almost all of Delaware, except for its northern tip, lie within the *Atlantic Coastal Plain*. The land is mostly flat, and lies at an elevation close to sea level. The region's rivers and creeks feed coastal *estuaries*, swamplands, and freshwater lakes. Among the major rivers are the Nanticoke, Choptank, and Pocomoke Rivers, which flow westward into the Chesapeake Bay. But most of Delaware's rivers, including the

 # Words to Understand in This Chapter

**Algonquian**—describing the language spoken by early Native American tribes living along the Atlantic Coast.

**Atlantic Coastal Plain**—a lowland, level region along the eastern seaboard extending 2,200 miles from New York to Florida.

**constitution**—a written document that contains the rules of a government.

**Delmarva**—a peninsula separating the Chesapeake Bay from the Atlantic Ocean that contains all of Delaware and parts of Maryland and Virginia.

**estuary**—the place where a freshwater stream or river meets the ocean; the mixing of fresh and ocean water results in slightly salty or brackish water.

**mill**—a building with machinery that grinds grain into flour or that is used in manufacturing processes.

**peninsula**—a strip of land surrounded on three sides by water.

**plain**—a large area of flat land with few trees.

**proprietor**—governor or holder of land.

**ratify**—to formally consent to a treaty or agreement, making it officially valid.

**semiautonomous**—having some, but not complete, self-government.

*Colorful foliage in Brandywine Creek State Park near Wilmington, just before sunset.*

Christina, Broadkill, and Indian, flow eastward into the Delaware Bay.

With its numerous small bays and inlets, Delaware has 381 miles (613 km) of shoreline, according to the National Oceanic and Atmospheric Administration (NOAA). The Atlantic coastline has sandy beaches that attract tourists, particularly in the summertime.

Delaware has a year-round moderate, although humid, climate. The average temperature in the summer is around 74° Fahrenheit (23° Celsius). The average winter temperature is 36°F (2°C). However, areas along the ocean coast tend to be about 10°F warmer in the winter and 10°F cooler in the summer compared to temperatures further inland. Annual precipitation is about 44 inches (112 centimeters) per year.

## History

For thousands of years various Native American cultures inhabited today's Delaware. By the 1400s, the Lenni Lenape, members of an *Algonquian*

*Henry Hudson was an English sea captain who was hired by the Dutch East India Company to find a westward route to Asia. During his 1609 voyage, he explored the Atlantic coast of what today is Delaware.*

group, had established numerous villages along the Delaware River. (The Europeans would later refer to the Lenni Lenape as the Delaware Indians.) Lenape hunted, fished, and tended crops such as beans, corn, and squash. Nearby Algonquian-speaking tribes in the south included the Nanticoke and Assateague.

In 1609 Englishman Henry Hudson, an explorer working for the Dutch East India Company, was the first European to discover the Delaware Bay and River. A year later, English sea captain Samuel Argall named the waters in honor of the governor of Virginia: Thomas West, Lord De La Warr.

Although these two men were English, it was the Dutch who established the first European settlement in the region. In 1631, a group of settlers under captain David Pietersz de Vries landed along the Delaware Bay, just inland from the Atlantic. The 28 men planned to set up a whaling colony. They named it Zwaanendael, which is Dutch for "valley of the swans." The following year, when de Vries returned to the site, he found the settlement had been destroyed by Native American tribes. All of the colonists were killed. About 25 years later, in 1659, the Dutch would return to area and refortify the old settlement. The resulting village would later be known as Lewes.

Another European country establishing colonies in the Delaware region was Sweden. In 1638 as a representative of the Swedish government, Peter Minuet dropped anchor in the Delaware River near Christina Creek, which the colonists had named in honor of the queen of Sweden. They also built an earthen fort in her name. Fort Christina became the first permanent European settlement in the Delaware Valley. It later became known as Wilmington.

The Dutch were not pleased by Sweden's claim. In 1651 they built Fort Casimir a few miles to the south of Fort Christina. A few years later, in 1655, the Dutch gained control of the region. They made Delaware a part of the growing colony they called New Netherland. By the mid 1600s the Dutch colony of New Netherland

*Replica of a settlers' log cabin at Fort Christina, located in what today is Wilmington. This Swedish colony, established in 1638, was named for the queen of Sweden. The Dutch took control of the colony in 1655. In 1664, control over the colony passed to English, which had gained all Dutch territories in North America.*

extended from Albany, New York, to Delaware.

The British also wanted to control the Delaware region. In 1644, they drove out the Dutch for the first time. Continued fighting saw the region exchange hands between the Dutch and British. But by 1682, the British had gained control, and Delaware officially became a British colony. However, its residents were not only English but also of Swedish, Dutch, and German descent.

The region known as "Three Lower Counties Upon Delaware" became part of the Pennsylvania colony, gov-

*The Immanuel Episcopal Church in New Castle is one of the oldest churches in North America. The parish was founded in 1689, and the church building was completed around 1708.*

erned by its *proprietor* William Penn. He called the three counties (from north to south) New Castle, Kent, and Sussex Counties.

In 1704 the Three Lower Counties became *semiautonomous* from Pennsylvania. This means the colony was allowed partial self-governance. The port town of New Castle, in the northern part of the colony, served as the new capital. There, four representatives from each county served as members of the Assembly of the Lower Counties. However, any laws they made had to be approved by the Pennsylvania governor.

During the 1700s disagreement over the boundary lines between the colony of Maryland, controlled by the Calvert family, and the Pennsylvania colony, governed by the Penn family, led to frequent fighting. The dispute was resolved by surveyors Charles Mason and Jeremiah Dixon. Their survey, completed in 1767, included the 83-mile (134 km) western border of today's Delaware.

Around the same time, growing dissatisfaction with British rule led the 13 American colonies to seek independence. Representatives from the Three Lower Counties supported the movement to separate from England. On June 15, 1776, members of Delaware's Colonial Assembly voted to cut all ties with England. This meant that they also separated from the proprietorship of the Penn family of Pennsylvania. The new colony of Delaware established the city of Dover as its capital.

About 4,000 soldiers from Delaware fought in the American War of Independence (1775–1783). The Delaware Regiment was noted for

 **Did You Know?**

During the Revolutionary War, the Delaware troops fought so well that they were given the nickname "Blue Hen's Chicken," after a breed of fighting gamecocks known for their ferocity. The blue hen is the state bird of Delaware. And it is the mascot for the athletic teams of the University of Delaware, located in Newark.

*Caesar Rodney (1728–1784) is best known for making an overnight ride of 70 miles (110 km) from Dover to the Continental Congress meeting in Philadelphia, where he cast the deciding vote on July 2 that authorized the Declaration of Independence.*

being well equipped and uniformed. Their short blue jackets, lined with red, white waistcoat, and buckskin breeches later became the standard uniform for all the Continental troops.

The only Revolutionary War battle on Delaware soil was the Battle of Cooch's Bridge, fought on September 3, 1777, near today's city of Newark. The newly created flag of the United States is said to have first flown in battle during the clash, which the British won. After the Battle of Brandywine on September 11, the British occupied the city of Wilmington for several months.

After achieving independence from England in 1783, the colonies strug-gled to establish a working government. Throughout the summer of 1787 delegates to the Constitutional Convention in Philadelphia worked to develop an acceptable framework. That September they signed the new U.S. Constitution, which required ratification by 9 of the 13 states. On December 7, 1787, Delaware became the first state to ratify the Constitution.

The 1800s saw the growth of agriculture in Delaware, with tobacco as an important crop. Rivers and streams powered numerous *mills*—buildings with machines that grind grains to make flour.

Mills also were used in the manufacture of gunpowder. In 1802 E. I. du Pont de Nemours and Company was founded when Éleuthère Irénée duPont de Nemours built gunpowder mills along the Brandywine River near

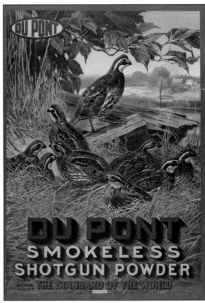

*The DuPont gunpowder mills were built on the Brandywine River and produced gunpowder from 1802 until 1921. They were closed due to the popularity of smokeless powder, which is produced using a different method. The poster on the right is from around 1913.*

Wilmington. Later in the 19th century the DuPont company produced explosives such as dynamite.

Wilmington soon became an industrial center. Other products such as cloth and paper were also produced in the city's many factories and mills. The completion in 1838 of a railroad linking Philadelphia and Baltimore that traveled through Wilmington also helped the city grow rapidly.

In the mid-1800s the issue of slavery led seven Southern states, whose plantation economies depended on slave labor, to secede from the Union. In 1861 they formed a separate nation called the Confederate States of America. The U.S. government, headed by President Abraham Lincoln, refused to accept this action. In 1861 civil war between the northern and the southern states broke out.

Slavery was not legal in most Northern states. In Delaware most black residents were free. However, slavery was legal. The state remained loyal to the U.S. government, and more than 12,000 troops from Delaware joined the Union forces. Only a few hundred joined the Confederate Army. The war cost hun-dreds of thousands of lives until it ended in 1865.

Troops from Delaware would par-ticipate in many more wars. From 1917 to 1918 nearly 10,000 Delawareans served in World War I. During World War II (1941–1945) 30,000 Delaware men and women served in the Armed Forces.

To defend against German sub-marines during World War II, the U.S. government established military posts on the Atlantic seaboard. In 1941 Fort Miles was built to guard the Delaware Bay and River shipping channels. Concrete observation towers, as well as battery casemates and bunkers, were built among the dunes of the Delaware coastline. These 11 observa-tion towers can still be seen today in the state parks of Cape Henlopen, Delaware Seashore, and Fenwick Island.

During the war, the civilian air-ports in Dover and New Castle were converted to military use. Dover Army Air Base, located two miles south of Delaware's capital city, is now known as Dover Air Force Base. New Castle

*This observation tower was part of the coastal defenses erected at Cape Henlopen and other spots along the Delaware Bay during World War II.*

Army Air Base later became New Castle Air National Guard Base.

Throughout the 1900s the northern region of Delaware benefitted from manufacturing jobs. The DuPont Company began producing industrial chemicals and synthetic fibers. Other products manufactured in Wilmington included textiles, paper, medical supplies, machinery, and automobiles. Wilmington had flour and textile mills as well as shipyards and iron foundries.

In 1981 the Delaware legislature passed laws that attracted financial institutions to Delaware. As a result, many banks and investment companies set up offices in northern Delaware, especially in Wilmington. The financial industry became an important employer in the state. Today, Wilmington is sometimes referred to as the Corporate Capital of the World.

*This control tower at Dover Air Force Base was opened in 2009. Dover Air Force Base covers more than 3,900 acres, has two runways, and 1,700 buildings.*

## Government

Delaware's current constitution was adopted in 1897. It calls for three branches of government: legislative (state senate and state house of representatives), executive (governor and state agencies), and judicial (courts). The business of government is conducted in the state capital of Dover.

## Did You Know?

Built in 1732, the New Castle Court House was Delaware's first court and state capitol. The building is one of the oldest surviving courthouses in the United States.

*Cupola atop the Delaware Legislative Hall in Dover, where the state assembly meets.*

The state's lawmaking, or legislative, body is called the Delaware General Assembly. This Assembly is comprised of the House of Representatives and a Senate. The State House of Representatives consists of 41 members elected to two-year terms, while the State Senate is made up of 21 Senators elected to four-year terms. There are no term limits. Sessions begin in January and end by June 30.

The executive branch is headed by the governor and lieutenant governor. Both serve four-year terms. They can be reelected only once.

The governor selects members of the highest judiciary body, the State Supreme Court. It is made up of a chief justice and four associate justices. The Senate must confirm the governor's appointments. Members of the State Supreme Court serve 12-year terms.

Delaware is represented by two senators in the U.S. Senate, and one representative in the U.S. House of Representatives. Delaware has three electoral votes in presidential elections.

*During the 1980s, Delaware passed several laws that created favorable conditions for large banking corporations to operate in the state. As a result, Wilmington has become home to many bank and credit card companies.*

## The Economy

Delaware's industry is concentrated in the north, in New Castle County. A major employer is DuPont Company, headquartered in Wilmington. Delaware's manufacturing products include chemicals, food products, rubber and plastics, paper products, synthetic fibers, and pharmaceuticals.

Since the 1990s the financial industry also has had a strong presence in northern Delaware. Credit card, investment, and tax-shelter businesses flocked to Delaware after state legislators cut bank taxes and liberalized loan rules in the 1980s.

During the 2000s Delaware saw the closing of several automobile plants. Up until then, the automotive industry had been a main contributor to the state's economy. However, while manufacturing declined, the number of jobs in the financial industry increased. Also of importance are insurance and real estate jobs. The massive Dover Air Force Base also provides jobs. It has been ranked as Delaware's third largest industry.

The two lower counties, Kent and Sussex, depend more upon agriculture. Major crops include corn, soybeans, barley, and wheat. Dairy farms and chicken houses dot the farmland. Processing plants produce chicken broilers and canned meats and vegetables. Major products from Delaware's fishing industry are crabs and clams.

Tourism has long been an important part of Delaware's economy. Among the popular attractions are Delaware beaches. Rehoboth Beach, Dewey Beach, and Fenwick Island are

*Lighthouse on the Delaware Bay at Cape Henlopen. This area was one of the first "public lands" in North America, as in 1682 William Penn declared it would be set aside for the use of citizens of Lewes and Sussex County.*

# Some Famous Delawareans

Joe Biden (b. 1942) who grew up in Claymont, Delaware, was at age 29 one of the youngest people elected to the U.S. Senate. In 2008 he became Vice President of the United States. His son, Beau Biden (b. 1969), born in Wilmington, is also a well-known politician in the state.

Henry Heimlich (b. 1920), a physician born in Wilmington, developed the Heimlich Maneuver to save choking victims.

Ruth Ann Minner (b. 1935), born in Sussex County, was the first woman elected governor of Delaware. She served two terms from 2000 to 2008. Prior to that she held elected office as a state representative, state senator, and lieutenant governor.

*Joe Biden*

Well-known artists of Delaware include Felix Darley (1822–1888) of Claymont, whose work illustrated many 19th-century novels, and artist and author Howard Pyle (1853–1911) of Wilmington.

Born in Wilmington, Mary Ann Shadd Cary (1823–1893) was an antislavery activist, publisher, and teacher. She also worked during the 19th century for woman's rights. An advocate for freedom and equality for all, she was the second black woman in the United States to earn a law degree.

*Ruth Ann Minner*

Boxing great Sugar Ray Leonard (b. 1941) of Wilmington was an Olympic boxing champion who won five gold medals.

Industrialist Éleuthère Irénée du Pont de Nemours (1771–1834) known as E.I. du Pont, emigrated from France to Wilmington in 1800. There, he founded a gunpowder company that grew into a billion-dollar industry. His descendants, members of the DuPont family, have played a significant role in U.S. politics and philanthropy during the 19th and 20th centuries.

*The University of Delaware in Newark enrolls about 16,000 undergraduate students.*

*Fans of speed can attend NASCAR races at Dover International Speedway, or horse races at Delaware Park near Wilmington.*

popular beach towns. Nearby recreation areas include Cape Henlopen, Delaware Seashore, and Trap Pond State Parks.

## The People

The 2010 U.S. Census showed that the population of Delaware increased by almost 15 percent since the previous census count taken in 2000. The number of residents in the state rose from 783,600 to 897,934. The greatest increase was in Kent County, which saw a population increase of 28 percent.

Most of Delaware's population is concentrated in the north around Wilmington, in New Castle County. Delaware is a densely populated state. In the 2010 Census the state ranked eighth in the nation in population density. (Population density refers to the number of people per square mile.) In Delaware there are 460.8 people per square mile.

Delaware's population is about 21 percent African American, 3 percent Asian and 68 percent white. From 2000 to 2010, the Hispanic population nearly doubled, from 37,273 in 2000 to 73,221 in 2010.

*Rehoboth Beach is a popular resort town in eastern Sussex County. It draws vacationers from Maryland, Virginia, Pennsylvania, and Washington, D.C.*

## Major Cities

*Wilmington* (pop. 70,851) is Delaware's largest city. It was founded in 1731 by Thomas Willing in the region where the Christina and

Delaware Rivers meet. The city is also the largest municipality on the Delmarva Peninsula. Formerly known as Willington, the town was renamed after the British gained control of the region. In 1739 it became Wilmington, in honor of Spencer Compton, Earl of Wilmington, a friend of the British king.

Attractions include the Hagley Museum (which was the first DuPont family home in the United States), the historical Holy Trinity Church (erected in 1698, the oldest house of worship in the United States still in use), the Fort Christina Monument, and the Winterthur Museum.

Located in Kent County, the state capital of **Dover** (pop. 36,047) is the site of most state government operations. It is the second-largest city in the state and the county seat of government as well. Dover Air Force Base is located in Dover. A major attraction is the Dover International Speedway.

About 12 miles west of Wilmington is **Newark** (pop. 31,454), the third-largest city in Delaware. It is home to the University of Delaware.

One of Delaware's fastest growing cities is **Middletown** (19,871). Located in New Castle County, its population grew by 206 percent from 2000 to 2010.

# Further Reading

Colbert, Judy. *Maryland and Delaware Off the Beaten Path: A Guide to Unique Places.* Guilford, Conn : Globe Pequot Press, 2010.

Cunningham, Kevin. *The Delaware Colony.* New York: Scholastic, 2011.

King, David C. *Delaware.* New York : Marshall Cavendish Benchmark, 2011.

# Internet Resources

**http://www.visitdelaware.com/**

Official tourism website of Delaware.

**http://www.delaware.gov/topics/facts/index.shtml**

This official web page includes information about important symbols as well as facts about Delaware.

**http://www.history.com/topics/us-states/delaware**

History Channel information about Delaware, including old photographs of the state.

**http://history.delaware.gov/**

The official website of the state of Delaware Division of Historical and Cultural Affairs has links to Museums and Historic Sites.

 # Text-Dependent Questions

1. What was the name of the first Dutch settlement in Delaware? When and where was it established and what happened to it?
2. Name five products of Delaware.
3. Which county of Delaware is the most densely populated?

 # Research Project

According to legend, U.S. president Thomas Jefferson referred to Delaware as a "jewel among states." As a result Delaware is nicknamed the "Diamond State." Using the Internet or your school library, find out why the nations third president considered Delaware to be so valuable. See if you can find first-hand accounts of Jefferson's quotation.

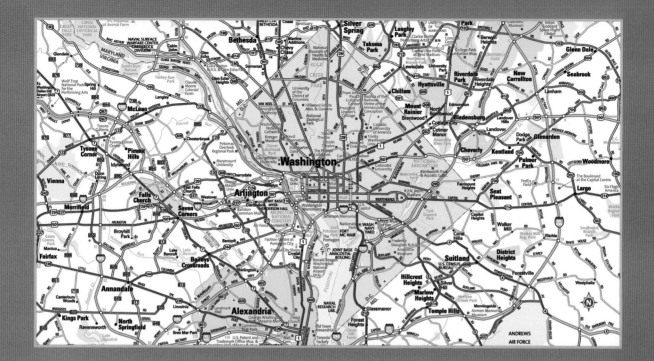

# Washington, D.C. at a Glance

**Area:** 68 sq miles (176 sq km)[1]
  *Land:* 61 sq mi (158 sq km)
  *Water:* 7 sq mi (18 sq km)
**Highest elevation:** Reno Reservoir in Tenleytown, 409 feet (125 m)
**Lowest elevation:** Potomac River (sea level)

**Statehood:** not a state
**Capital:** serves as the U.S. capital

**Population:** 658,893[2]

**Nicknames:** D.C.; the Capital City
**Official bird:** wood thrush
**Official flower:** American beauty rose

[1] *U.S. Census Bureau*
[2] *U.S. Census Bureau, 2014 estimate*

# District of Columbia

With its low buildings and wide sunny streets, Washington, D.C., welcomes all visitors. They are drawn to the capital city's many monuments and museums, which have made the District of Columbia (D.C.), as the city is known, one of the most popular *metropolitan* areas in the world. But the District is much more than a tourist attraction. As the nation's center of government, the capital city represents the wealth and power of the United States of America.

## Geography

The District of Columbia lies on the north bank of the Potomac River and covers an area of just 68 square miles. It is bordered by Maryland to the north and Virginia to the south. Two tributaries feed the Potomac—the Anacostia River and Rock Creek. Another tributary, the Tiber Creek, once flowed in the region, heading westward to the Potomac River. But in 1880 it was enclosed as an underground sewer. Today it is hidden, running underneath the city's Constitution Avenue to the Potomac.

The District consists mostly of low flat land. There are some higher elevations. One is a small rise in the center of the city, where the U.S. Congress meets in the Capitol Building. This elevated area is known as Capitol Hill. The city's highest elevation is in the northwest. Point Marina in Fort Reno Park stands 409 feet (125 m) above sea level. The lowest elevation is sea level along the Potomac River.

About 20 percent of D.C. is parkland. The city's largest park is in the northwestern part of the District. Rock Creek Park extends about 9 miles along Rock Creek, which flows south. Another large park area is the Chesapeake and Ohio (C&O) Canal National Historical Park. Managed by the National Park Service, the park runs from the D.C. neighborhood of Georgetown to Cumberland Maryland. The 184.5-mile (297 km) canal and towpath that parallel the Potomac River served as an important waterway during the 1800s.

The District of Columbia has a temperate, or mild, climate. Winter

# Words to Understand in This Chapter

**federal**—relating to the central government of a united federation of states.

**government contractor**—a private company that produces goods or services under contract for the government.

**home rule**—self government.

**lobby**—to seek to influence the decisions made by a public official regarding an issue or political decision.

**metropolitan**—describing a large densely populated city and its surrounding suburbs.

**retrocede**—to give territory back.

**secede**—officially withdraw from a union of states.

*Rock Creek Park is a 2,000 acre (809 ha) natural area in the northwestern part of the District.*

temperatures average around 38°F (3°C). Summers are typically hot and humid. In July the average temperature is around 80°F (27°C). Average annual precipitation is about 40 inches (102 cm).

## History

The area that makes up the District of Columbia was originally part of southern Maryland. And before becoming part of Maryland, the region had been home to various Native American chiefdoms. The Algonquian-speaking Piscataway Indians inhabited much of the area.

In the 1600s, when European explorers arrived, they found hundreds of established villages, often along waterfronts. Fur traders were among the first Europeans to learn about the land and its people. In 1632 Henry Fleet established a trading post on the Potomac River. He learned

*George Washington was the first president of the United States elected after ratification of the U.S. Constitution. During his presidency (1789–1800), New York was the capital city of the new nation. However, Washington spent a good deal of time planning the new federal district, as well as the city that would eventually bear his name.*

enough of the Algonquian language that he could help the first colonists from England buy land from the native people. In 1634 the Yaocomaco sold their village to the English who founded St. Mary's City. Other settlements followed. They included the port town of Georgetown, founded on the Potomac in 1751.

During the mid-1700s many American colonists began to object to British rule. In September 1774 they formed the first Continental Congress. Delegates from 12 of the 13 colonies made up the Congress, which met in Philadelphia. The Congress called on England to address their grievances.

But less than a year later, hostilities began. In April 1775, fighting broke out at Lexington and Concord, Massachusetts. Two months later the Second Continental Congress chose George Washington of Virginia to lead the Continental Army against the British. In July 1776, the Continental Congress officially declared independence from British rule.

The American Revolutionary War lasted seven years. In October 1781 the British surrender in Yorktown, Virginia, was an important victory. But the war did not officially end until 1783, when the British and Americans

*This British illustration from 1803 shows the rural nature of Washington, D.C., at that time.*

signed a peace treaty. And a new nation was born.

By 1789 the U.S. Constitution, which established a *federal*, or central, government, had been ratified. The Constitution called for a "federal district" that would not be under the authority of any state. This district would serve as the seat of government. In July 1790 Congress passed the Residence Act, defined the district as a ten-mile square territory. George Washington chose a site for the new federal capital along the Potomac River, between Virginia and Maryland. And in 1791 an amendment to the Act

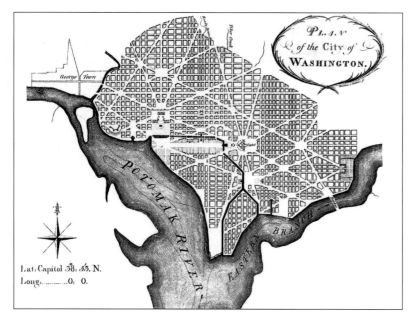

*The original plan for Washington, D.C., produced by Pierre L'Enfant and based on surveys done by Andrew Ellicott and his Baltimore-born assistant, Benjamin Banneker (below).*

approved the location chosen by Washington.

The 10-mile by 10-mile square of land set aside for the capital was turned so it formed a diamond shape. The states of Maryland and Virginia each contributed territory for it. The resulting district included the port towns of Alexandria, Virginia, and Georgetown, Maryland.

From 1791 to 1792, surveyor Andrew Ellicott and his assistants, who included a free African-American astronomer and mathematician named Benjamin Banneker, surveyed the borders of the new federal district. To mark the boundary they placed large sandstone rocks at one-mile intervals. Most of these 40 boundary stones remain today and are considered the oldest federal monuments.

Washington chose three commissioners to oversee the surveying, design, and construction of the capital city. The commissioners hired French-born architect Pierre Charles L'Enfant to design it. And they decided that the city should be named Washington, in honor of the country's first president. George Washington had named the territory the District of Columbia, in honor of explorer Christopher Columbus.

The city plan developed by L'Enfant was inspired by the broad streets and avenues of Paris. L'Enfant devised a grid street pattern broken up in places by rectangles. He divided the city into four sections: Northwest, Southwest, Northeast and Southeast. And he had the U.S. Capitol building marks point of the city where the four quadrants meet.

Although his plan was used, L'Enfant did not oversee its completion. After many disagreements with the three commissioners, he was dismissed. Other architects were hired to design the Capitol Building, White House, and other public buildings.

Construction began in 1793. President John Adams and his wife Abigail moved into the White House in November 1800. That same month the first session of Congress was held in the U.S. Capitol, even though the building was still under construction. By 1801 Washington, D.C., had officially replaced Philadelphia as the nation's capital.

The city was still under construction 13 years later, when many of its buildings were destroyed during the War of 1812. This three-year conflict between Great Britain and the United States resulted in the only time Washington was occupied by enemy forces. On the night of August 24, 1814 British forces invaded the city.

*The White House, located at 1600 Pennsylvania Avenue NW in Washington, D.C., is the official residence and principal office of the president of the United States. The only president who did not live there was George Washington.*

In a raid that became known as the Burning of Washington, they set fire to public and government buildings.

British occupation of the city lasted only a day. The enemy troops retreated to their ships on August 25, when a fierce thunderstorm ripped through the city. The rains put out most of the fires and the sandstone walls of the White House and Capitol remained intact. The White House was repaired by 1817. The Capitol, which had still been under construction, would not be completed until 1868.

By that time the District had lost its diamond shape. The land donated by Virginia, which included the city of Alexandria and Alexandria County (now Arlington County) had been *retroceded* to Virginia in 1846. The issue of slavery factored in the decision to reduce the district by a third. Virginia was a slave state, and businessmen in the port town of Alexandria did not want to be part of the District. They were concerned that the District would outlaw slavery.

Slavery would not be abolished in Washington, D.C., until 1862. That

*Peirce Mill, a water-powered grist mill, was built in the 1820s. Today, it is a historical museum that is open to the public and operated by the National Park Service.*

year President Abraham Lincoln signed the Compensated Emancipation Act. It ended slavery in the District of Columbia and granted freedom to more than 3,000 slaves.

Meanwhile, the United States was immersed in a bloody civil war (1860–1865). The Northern states opposed slavery, while the Southern states sought to continue the institution. Rejecting efforts to abolish slavery, seven southern states **seceded** from the Union. They formed a new government, the Confederate States of America. The United States, or Union, led by President Abraham

*View of Washington, D.C., as it appeared in 1863. The open area at the upper right is what today is known as the National Mall. The large structure is the Smithsonian Castle, which was built in 1855 and originally housed the museum collection. Over time, other museums would be built adjacent to the Castle, and numerous monuments would be erected on the Mall. (To the right of the Castle, toward the Potomac River, the lower portion of the unfinished Washington Monument is faintly visible.)*

Lincoln, refused to accept the new nation. Civil War broke out on April 12, 1861, when Confederate forces fired on Union troops at Fort Sumter, in South Carolina.

Before the Civil War, Washington had been a small city with a population of about 75,000. During the course of the war, the city population tripled to more than 200,000. More than 40,000 newcomers were freed and runaway slaves, who fled to Washington after the Compensated Emancipation Act of 1862 went into effect. Hundreds of thousands more were Union soldiers, who established military camps in and around the city.

Confederate troops continually threatened the city. To protect the District President Lincoln ordered the construction of fortifications and forts. Eventually a 37-mile ring of 68 earthen forts with cannon batteries and rifle pits were built. At the same time new government buildings, hospitals, and roads were built to accommodate the growing population.

Despite the threat of attack, Washington city limits were broached only once. On July 11, 1864, the

*U.S. soldiers stand at attention next to the Capitol building in Washington, D.C., during the Civil War. The legislative branch of the U.S. government (the Senate and House of Representatives) meets in the Capitol building. Originally built in 1800, the structure has been expanded several times.*

Confederate army led by General Jubal Early skirmished with Union forces during the two-day Battle of Fort Stevens. The rebel troops were repelled, although more than 900 soldiers were killed or wounded on both sides.

More than 620,000 Americans died during the U.S. Civil War. The conflict ended in April 1865 with the surrender of Confederate general Robert E. Lee. That same month, President Abraham Lincoln was assassinated in Washington, D.C., by John Wilkes Booth.

In 1871, during the presidency of Ulysses S. Grant, Congress passed the Organic Act. It repealed the individual charters of the cities of Washington and Georgetown, making them a single municipality. And it established a new territorial government for the entire District of Columbia. Three years later, in 1874, Congress established a board consisting of three commissioners to govern the city.

After the war, the city of Washington continued to grow. By 1900 its population was about 279,000. In the 1930s, during the

 **Did You Know?**

Completed in 1884, the Washington Monument on the National Mall is the world's tallest freestanding stone structure. Because of a 1910 federal law restricting building height, no building in the District of Columbia may be taller than 130 feet (40 m). As a result the Monument, which stands 555 feet (169 m) high, is the city's tallest structure.

severe economic downturn of the Great Depression, people were drawn to Washington by the promise of work. President Franklin D. Roosevelt had addressed the economic decline with New Deal programs that provided jobs. During World War II (1941–1945) there were many jobs in wartime Washington. By 1950 D.C. had reached a peak population of 802,178 residents.

As the nation's capital, Washington became the place for people to make their voices heard through protest marches. In the 1910s and 1920s women marched for the right to vote.

*Lafayette Park, across from the White House, has become a popular spot for those who want to protest against government policies, such as these activists who are seeking immigration reform.*

In the 1930s war veterans demanded overdue bonuses from President Herbert Hoover. During the 1960s African Americans called for civil rights. A major civil rights demonstration took place on August 1963 on the National Mall. The March on Washington for Jobs and Freedom was a peaceful protest calling for equal rights for African Americans. The Mall was also the site during the 1960s of many anti-Vietnam War demonstrations.

In 1973, after almost 100 years under an appointed commission sys-tem, residents of the District gained the right to elect local representatives to govern themselves. That year Congress enacted the District of Columbia *Home Rule* Act. D.C. residents could elect a mayor and 13-member council to govern the District. When elections were held in 1975 Walter Washington became the first mayor.

This form of home rule is not enough for some residents. Some of them have worked for decades to make D.C. a state. One advocacy group had success in May 2014 in getting 17 senators to jointly sponsor a bill for statehood. The bill would make part of the District a 51st state called New Columbia. Some people question whether such legislation is lawful since it disregards the language in the U.S. Constitution calling for a federal district that is not under the control of any state.

## Government

There are no counties in the District of Columbia. And there is just one city—Washington. The city of Washington is legally regarded as the same as the District of Columbia.

As the nation's capital, Washington, D.C., houses all three branches of the federal government. The executive branch is represented by the White House, the legislature by the Capitol building, and the judiciary by the Supreme Court building.

Since 1975 the city itself has been governed by a locally elected mayor and 13-member council. Eight of the council members are elected from each of the city's eight wards. Four are elected as at-large representatives.

## Did You Know?

The Capitol Hill neighborhood is the largest historic neighborhood in Washington, D.C.

That is, they represent the entire district. Still, by U.S. law (Article One, Section Eight of the United States Constitution) Congress holds final jurisdiction over the District. Congress has the power to overturn any laws created by the council.

*Marion Barry served as mayor of Washington, D.C., from 1979 to 1991, when he decided not to run after being arrested for using drugs. After spending six months in a federal prison, Barry was re-elected as mayor and served from 1995 to 1999.*

## Did You Know?

On August 23, 2011, an earthquake centered in Virginia damaged several structures in the District. The Washington Monument, the main train station (Union Station), and the National Cathedral received significant damage.

D.C. citizens do not have full representation in Congress. They can elect a delegate to the U.S. House of Representatives. And this person can vote in committee and draft legislation. However, he or she cannot vote on any bills. Residents also elect two so-called shadow senators and a shadow representative. This shadow delegation cannot vote with the legislature. But it lobbies Congress on District issues and concerns.

Since 1961, D.C. residents have had a voice in presidential elections. That year, the Twenty-third Amendment to the U.S. Constitution was ratified. It gives three electoral votes to the District.

## The Economy

The federal government is a major employer in the Washington metropolitan area. But it is not the largest single employer. It accounts for only about 13 percent of jobs. State and local government jobs account for another 12 percent of jobs in the metropolitan area.

About 15 percent of the workforce is employed in professional, scientific, and technical services. There are also many high tech and bioscience enterprises based in Washington. Other important industries include businesses that work in research, medicine, publishing, and international finance. The early 2010s have seen job growth in services such as leisure and hospitality, health care, education, and finance and insurance.

As the nation's government center, D.C. attracts groups and organizations looking to establish contact with or influence the federal government. They include foreign embassies and international organizations, *lobbying* firms, professional trade associations, and defense and civilian **government contractors**. The large number of businesses with ties to federal government has resulted in a strong, stable economy in Washington. The District has one of the lowest rates of unemployment in the nation.

Tourism is also a major industry in Washington D.C. In 2012 the U.S. Department of Commerce reported a record 18.5 visitors spent time and money in the District.

Tourists visit the Lincoln Memorial in Washington, D.C.

## The People

More than half a million people are residents of Washington, D.C. However, during the workweek, the city population grows to more than a million when commuters from the adjacent states of Maryland and Virginia come to work.

The 2010 U.S. Census reported that the city's population is 601,723. This was an increase from 2000, when the District had a population of 572,059. In 2010 the racial makeup was about 38 percent white, 51 percent African American, 4 percent Asian, and 6 percent other or two or more races. Hispanics made up 9.1 percent of the D.C. population.

## Major Attractions

Tourism is a major part of the D.C. economy. And at the top of most visitors' lists are the city's National Mall and Memorial Parks.

Located between the Lincoln Memorial and the U.S. Capitol building, the National Mall is a large open park. Over the years the green space has served as a site for political protests, festivals, and concerts—as

# Famous People of Washington, D.C.

Born in Washington, D.C., John Foster Dulles (1888–1959), served as the U.S. secretary of state in the 1950s during the Eisenhower Administration. The Washington Dulles International Airport, located in Northern Virginia is named in his honor.

Washington-born John Edgar Hoover (1895–1972) served as director of the Federal Bureau of Investigation.

Former U.S. Senator, vice president, and 2000 presidential nominee Al Gore (b. 1948) was born in the District of Columbia.

The first African American to hold a cabinet rank, Robert C. Weaver (1907–1997), served as secretary of housing and urban development during the administration of President Lyndon B. Johnson.

*Robert C. Weaver*

Civil rights activist Walter E. Fauntroy (b. 1933) served as the District's first delegate to Congress when the office was reestablished in 1971. He was born and raised in the District. D.C. native Eleanor Holmes Norton (b. 1937) replaced him as the District of Columbia member of the House of Representatives in 1991.

Helen Hayes (1900–1993) began her acting career at age 5 and retired at age 85. The annual Helen Hayes Award, which recognizes excellence in professional theater in the Washington, D.C., area, honors her. Other D.C.-born performers include William Hurt (b. 1950), Samuel L. Jackson (b. 1948), and Dave Chappelle (b. 1973).

Charles R. Drew (1904–1950) was an African-American physician and medical researcher in the fields of blood plasma and blood transfusions. He developed the blood bank concept.

Jazz pianist, composer, and bandleader Edward Kennedy "Duke" Ellington (1899–1974) was born and raised in Washington's Shaw neighborhood. Other famous Washingtonian-born musicians include bandmaster and composer John Philip Sousa (1854–1932) and Motown recording artist Marvin Gaye (1939–1984).

well as presidential inaugurations. Numerous memorials can be found on the Mall. They include one of the city's oldest—the Washington Monument, a 555-foot marble obelisk completed in 1885. Newer memorials include the Franklin Delano Roosevelt Memorial, which opened in 1997, and the Martin Luther King, Jr. Memorial, dedicated in 2011. Other monuments include the Lincoln Memorial and Reflecting Pool, the Thomas Jefferson Memorial, the National World War II Memorial, the Korean War Veterans Memorial, and the Vietnam Veterans Memorial.

The buildings that house the workings of the federal government also attract visitors. They can tour the

*Georgetown University is one of the nation's top private universities. The school was founded in 1789, and is the oldest Jesuit and Roman Catholic university in the United States. About 7,000 undergraduate and 10,000 graduate students are enrolled at Georgetown.*

*Entrance to the National Zoological Park.*

White House, the Capitol Building House and Senate Galleries, and the U.S. Supreme Court. Another attraction located on Capitol Hill is the three-building complex that makes up the Library of Congress.

The Smithsonian Institution is a big part of Washington. It is named for James Smithson (1765–1829), a British scientist, who left the U.S. government his estate to be used for "the increase and diffusion of knowledge." The red sandstone brick headquarters of the educational foundation, known as "The Castle," was built on the National Mall in 1855. As of 2014 the Smithsonian consists of 19 museums, the National Zoo and nine research facilities. The museums and zoo are open to the public free of charge. Among the most visited Smithsonian museums are the National Museum of Natural History and the Air and Space Museum. The Smithsonian museums and the zoo attract millions of visitors each year.

# Further Reading

Chernick, Miriam. *A Kid's Guide to Washington, D.C.* Boston: Houghton Mifflin Harcourt Books for Young Readers, 2008.

House, Katherine L. *The White House for Kids: A History of a Home, Office, and National Symbol, with 21 Activities.* Chicago Review Press, 2014.

Kent, Deborah. *Washington, D.C.* New York: Children's Press, 2010.

Ogintz, Eileen. *The Kid's Guide to Washington, D.C.* Guilford, Conn: Globe Pequot, 2013.

# Internet Resources

**www.dc.gov**

The official website of the government of the District of Columbia.

**http://washington.org/topics/history-heritage**

History and heritage information from the official Washington, D.C., tourism website.

**http://www.nps.gov/nacc/index.htm**

This website with information about the National Mall and Memorial Parks in Washington, D.C., is managed by the National Park Service.

 # Text-Dependent Questions

1. How did Washington, D.C., get its name?
2. What are the three main branches of the federal government? What buildings in Washington, D.C., are associated with each branch?
3. Why don't Washingtonians have a vote in Congress?

 # Research Project

Washington, D.C., is the place where people often gather to make their voices heard through protests and rallies. Choose one of the following demonstrations or one approved by your teacher, look up information about the event in your school library or on the Internet, and write a one-page report about it:

• March 1913, Woman Suffrage March
• June 1932, Bonus Army March
• August 1963, March on Washington for Jobs and Freedom
• November 1969, March to End the War in Vietnam
• October 1995, Million Man March
• September 2009, Taxpayer March on Washington

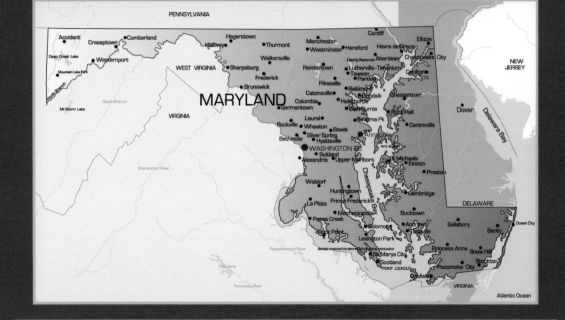

# Maryland at a Glance

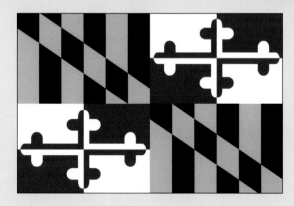

**Area:** 12,406 sq miles (32,132 sq km). 42nd largest state[1]
*Land:* 9,707 sq mi (25,141 sq km)
*Water:* 2,699 sq mi (6,990 sq km)
**Highest elevation:** Hoye Crest, 3,360 feet (1,024 m)
**Lowest elevation:** Atlantic Ocean (sea level)

**Statehood:** April 28, 1788 (7th state)
**Capital:** Annapolis

**Population:** 5,976,407 (19th largest state)[2]

**State nicknames:** Old Line State, The Free State
**State bird:** Baltimore Oriole
**State flower:** Black-eyed Susan

[1] *U.S. Census Bureau*
[2] *U.S. Census Bureau, 2014 estimate*

# Maryland

Located along the East Coast, the state of Maryland can be described as America in miniature. Although small in area, the state has many geographical features found in the United States. It has sandy beaches and coastal plains. And it also has lakes, forested plateaus, rolling foothills, and mountains. Maryland may be small, but it has a lot to offer!

## Geography

Maryland is bordered by Pennsylvania to the north, West Virginia to the west, Virginia and Washington, D.C., to the south, and Delaware and the Atlantic Ocean to the east. The Potomac River lies along its southern boundary. And the Chesapeake Bay divides Maryland into two regions referred to as the Eastern Shore and Western Shore.

The state has three major geographical sections. Western Maryland is features higher elevations of the Appalachian Mountains. This mountainous region gently slopes eastward to the more level forest-

*A waterfall in the wooded Catoctin Mountains, part of the Appalachian range in Maryland.*

ed **Piedmont** Plateau of central Maryland. Further east lies the Atlantic Coastal Plain, with flat low marshlands and sandy dunes that border the Atlantic Ocean.

Maryland is laced with rivers, bays, and creeks that feed into the Chesapeake Bay. These waterways help make up the *watershed* of the Bay—a watershed is an area of land in which all water on or under the land drains to one common place. The watershed of the Chesapeake Bay extends through the District of Columbia and New York, Pennsylvania, Delaware, Maryland, West Virginia, and Virginia. Some major Maryland rivers that flow into

# Words to Understand in This Chapter

**charter**—a written grant given by the king, in which exclusive powers for governing land are given to a proprietor or a settlement company.

**piedmont**—a gentle slope leading from the base of mountains to a region of flat land; a plateau region.

**watershed**—an area of land in which all water on or under the land drains to one common place.

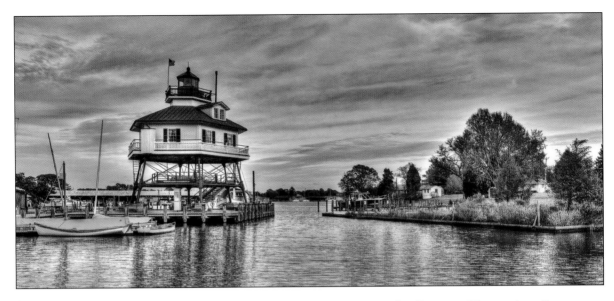

*The Drum Point Light, built in 1883, is located at the point where the Patuxent River enters the Chesapeake Bay.*

the Chesapeake Bay are the Patapsco, Patuxent, and Susquehanna Rivers.

Although there are many rivers and creeks, Maryland has no natural lakes. But more than 100 have been created by damming waterways. The largest is Deep Creek Lake, located in western Maryland's Garrett County. It covers almost 4,000 acres (1,619 ha) and has 65 miles (105 km) of shoreline.

But Maryland's greatest waterway is the Chesapeake Bay. It is 195 miles (314 km) long and has shorelines in both Maryland and Virginia. The Bay varies from 3 to 20 miles (5 to 32 km) wide and covers approximately 1,726 square miles (4,470 sq km). The Chesapeake Bay is the largest estuary in the United States. The brackish, water provides a habitat for a large variety of fish, shellfish and crabs. In Maryland the Bay is home to Atlantic menhaden, striped bass, Eastern oyster, and the Blue crab.

*In 1989 the Maryland Blue Crab was designated the State Crustacean.*

Like its varying topography, the climate of Maryland changes depending upon location. In the more mountainous western regions, temperatures have dropped as low as -40°F (-40°C) in the winter and risen as high as 109°F (43°C) in the summer. Average temperatures are about 65°F (18°C) in July and 28°F (-2°C) in January. The Piedmont and Coastal Plain regions of Maryland usually have more moderate temperatures. Average temperatures in July are 75°F (24°C) and in January 35°F (2°C). However, there is often high humidity during summer months. Annual precipitation is about 41 inches (104 cm).

## History

Maryland's first inhabitants were Native Americans, who lived in the region for thousands of years. When European explorers arrived in the 1600s, they found large numbers of established villages dotted the shores of the region's rivers and bays. These native Americans lived off of turkey, fish, and oysters, and crops of corn, squash, and beans.

In the 1600s the most powerful chiefdom on Maryland's Western Shore was that of the Piscataway. Between 1607 and 1609 John Smith

 **Did You Know?**

The Native American chiefdoms on the lower Eastern Shore included the Assateagues along the Atlantic shore, as well as the Pocomoke along the Pocomoke River. Other chiefdoms for which rivers are named in Maryland include the Manokin, Nanticoke, and Choptank.

and a crew of men exploring the Chesapeake Bay, visited many of their villages. Smith came from the newly established English colony in Jamestown, Virginia, which is about 150 miles south of the Bay. He mapped nearly 3,000 miles (4,800 km) of the Bay and rivers, and also kept journals describing the native people.

England laid claim to the explored lands. And in 1632 King Charles I granted a *charter* making George Calvert, Lord Baltimore, proprietor. After his son Cecilius Calvert inherited the vast holdings, he became proprietor. Calvert organized an expedition to establish a colony. He called the territory Maryland in honor of Henrietta Maria, the queen. And he named his brother Leonard as governor.

In March 1634 the first colonists arrived. The newcomers paid the Algonquian-speaking Yaocomaco Indians for their village on the north bank of the Potomac River on Maryland's Western Shore. There, the English group founded the town of St. Mary's City. It would eventually serve as the seat of the colonial government.

The Yaocomaco and nearby Piscataway tribes welcomed the colonists at first. But they had not been exposed to many of the diseases carried by the Europeans. With no immunological protection, many Native Americans died. The remainder left the area to establish new villages further north.

Many colonists came to Maryland in search of religious freedom. In the 1630s Catholics in England were being persecuted. In England they

*Colonists with the flag of the Calvert family arrive in present-day Maryland. The colonial town of St. Mary's City is now a state-owned archaeological site and living history museum.*

*Baltimore is the largest city in Maryland. More than 600,000 people live in the city itself, with over 2 million more living in the metropolitan area surrounding Baltimore. This view of the downtown skyline shows the Inner Harbor, a former industrial area that was redeveloped during the 1970s and 1980s to attract tourists.*

were expected to be loyal only to the King's religion, the Church of England. However, in Maryland, all Christian religions were protected. People could practice their faith and hold public office—something they could not do in England at the time.

The first European colonists established estates for growing tobacco. Workers were typically indentured servants. These were poor people who signed a contract agreeing to work for a set period of time for the person who paid their way to the New World. Once the debt was paid, indentured servants received land or money. This allowed them to own and farm their own property. By the late 1600s, fewer people were willing to become indentured servants. Tobacco growers turned to slave labor, using African people who had been kidnapped and brought by force across the Atlantic Ocean.

Sometime the charters granted for colonies conflicted. Members of the Penn family, proprietors of the Pennsylvania colony, and the Calverts, who controlled Maryland, battled over the boundary lines of the two colonies.

The land dispute was resolved in 1767 when surveyors Charles Mason and Jeremiah Dixon completed a boundary survey begun in 1763. The two surveyors marked off a 233-mile-long straight line dividing Maryland and Pennsylvania (which at the time also included the colony of Delaware). The Mason-Dixon line became the official boundary with Pennsylvania.

In 1776 Maryland joined the American colonies in declaring independence from Britain. Many Maryland citizens joined the fight against England during the Revolutionary War (1775–1783). After the American colonies won their independence, the Maryland city of Annapolis served for a short time as the capital of the newly created United States. The Continental Congress met there from November 1783 to June 1784.

It took several years for the country's Founding Fathers to develop a workable constitution for the new nation. In September 1787 they signed the new U.S. Constitution. To become law, it had to be ratified by nine of the 13 states. On April 28, 1788, Maryland became the seventh

*Charles Carroll (1737–1832) was a wealthy landowner and influential political leader from Maryland. He was the only Roman Catholic to sign the Declaration of Independence, and served in both the legislature created by the Articles of Confederation and as a senator in the U.S. Congress.*

of the 13 colonies to ratify the document. By 1789 the U.S. Constitution had been ratified. Two years later, Maryland ceded part of its southern territory for the new "federal district" that would serve as the seat of government for the new nation.

Maryland's central position on the eastern seaboard proved an ideal location for trade by ship. And with its many bays and waterways, the state developed a strong shipbuilding industry. By the early 1800s, Maryland's port city of Baltimore had become an important center of commerce. It was also Maryland's largest city.

Around that time the United States declared war again against

*Left) Aerial view of Fort McHenry, which defended Baltimore harbor from a British invasion in September 1814. (Right) After watching the battle from the deck of a British warship, Francis Scott Key wrote a poem that would become our National Anthem, "The Star-Spangled Banner."*

Great Britain. During the three-year War of 1812 many battles took place on U.S. soil. Some of these conflicts occurred in Maryland. One was the Battle of Bladensburg, which took place on August 24, 1814. British troops routed thousands of American militiamen from the town of Bladensburg, which is outside the capital city of Washington, D.C. The British went on to occupy Washington, D.C. They looted and burned major public buildings before withdrawing on August 26. Hours before the British arrived, President James Madison fled to Brookeville, Maryland. The small town later claimed the distinction of serving as the U.S. capital for a day.

Another important battle was the British naval attempt to capture the port city of Baltimore. On the evening of September 13, 1814, the British began bombarding nearby Fort

McHenry. The nighttime bombardment inspired Francis Scott Key to write the words to the "Star Spangled Banner."

A half a century later the United States would again be at war. In 1860 disagreements over slavery ignited the Civil War. The Mason-Dixon Line symbolically marked the Northern free states from the Southern slave-holding states. Although Maryland was south of the line and a slave-holding state, it did not join the Confederacy. The majority of men from Maryland joined the Union forces, while about one fourth enlisted with the Confederate army. Maryland residents were divided in their support for Confederate and Union soldiers.

During the war, two major battles took place in Maryland. September 17, 1862, saw the first attack on Union soil. The opposing forces—the Confederate Army and Union troops met in a bloody confrontation in Sharpsburg, along the Antietam Creek. The fighting ended in a stalemate, although the Confederate forces led by General Robert E. Lee were turned back. Antietam came to be known as the bloodiest single day of the war. In one day 23,000 men were killed, wounded, or missing.

A second key Civil War fight in Maryland was the July 9, 1864, Battle of Monocacy. The Monocacy River is a tributary of the Potomac River. In another attempt to invade the North, Confederate troops led General Jubal Early invaded Maryland. His goal was to capture the city of Washington. On July 9, when his forces were south of

*The bodies of Confederate soldiers lie near a church shortly after the battle at Antietam. Shortly after this Union victory, President Lincoln issued the Emancipation Proclamation, declaring that all slaves in rebellious states would be freed on January 1, 1863.*

Frederick on the banks of the Monocacy, they met up with troops led by Union general Lew Wallace. Although Early's troops defeated the Union forces, the delay foiled his plan to take the capital city. The Battle of Monocacy is also known as "The Battle That Saved Washington."

War was still raging in November 1864, when a new Maryland constitution became law. Included in the document was the abolition of slavery. Because the former slave state outlawed slavery, Maryland earned the nickname "the Free State." The Civil War ended in April 1865 with the surrender of Confederate general Robert E. Lee.

After the war the city of Baltimore grew and thrived. Its seaport and railroad lines such as the Baltimore and Ohio (B&O) railroad had drawn businesses to the city before the war. After the war more manufacturing industries chose Baltimore and the surrounding area to do business.

These industrial jobs attracted job seekers from Europe. Baltimore became the third largest point of entry for European immigrants. During the 1840s many of these immigrants came from Ireland. But after the Civil War and during the first half of the 20th century most were from Russia, Poland, and Italy.

As a manufacturing center, Baltimore contributed a great deal to war production during World War II. Of major significance was the manufacture of Liberty ships, which carried cargo needed for the war effort, and military aircraft. After the war, however, Baltimore fell into an economic

The U.S. Naval Academy in Annapolis was founded in 1845. Its mission is to develop officers "morally, mentally, and physically" for service in the Navy or Marine Corps.

decline as jobs in the steel industry and textile and manufacturing vanished. In 1950 Baltimore had a population of 950,000. But from 1950 to 2000, many residents left the city and moved to the suburbs.

Although the city of Baltimore lost residents, Maryland did not. The population of the state continued to grow during the 20th and early 21st centuries.

*The Maryland State House in Annapolis is the oldest state capitol building still in continuous use.*

## Government

The current constitution of Maryland was adopted in September 1867. It calls for a state government structured like that of the federal government: There are three branches: executive, legislative, and judiciary. Government business takes place in the state capital of Annapolis.

The executive branch is headed by the governor, who is elected to a four-year term. He or she cannot serve more than two terms. Since 1970 a lieutenant governor has also served the state. The executive branch includes departments responsible for oversight of agriculture, education, community development, state police, transportation, and other areas.

The Maryland General Assembly is the legislative branch, tasked with making laws. The Assembly consists of the Maryland Senate and the Maryland House of Delegates. The Maryland Senate consists of 47 members who serve 4-year terms and represent one of the state's 47 legislative districts. There are 141 members in the House of Delegates, with three elected from each of the 47 districts. They also serve four-year terms. The General Assembly meets each year beginning in January for 90 days.

The judicial branch of Maryland's state government is the state court system that applies and interprets laws. Each of Maryland's 23 counties, plus Baltimore City, has its own court system. When a person opposes a ruling at this local level, he or she can appeal to a higher court. The highest court in Maryland is the Court of Appeals.

In the U.S. Senate, Maryland is represented by two senators, who serve six-year terms. In the U.S. House of Representative, there are eight representatives. Every two years, voters elect one representative from each of Maryland's eight congressional districts. Maryland voters participating in national presidential elections have 10 electoral votes

## The Economy

Most Marylanders—about 82 percent—work in the service industry. Their jobs may deal with services in the community; wholesale and retail trade; government; finance, insurance and real estate; or transportation and utilities. Just 9 percent of Marylanders hold jobs in manufacturing, 7 percent work in construction, and 2 percent in agriculture.

Twenty percent of Marylanders work in government services at the federal, state, county and municipal levels. Many Maryland residents work for the federal government in offices located in the District of Columbia. Others have jobs in federal institutions or government agencies located in Maryland. The latter include the National Institutes of Health, the National Institute of Standards and Technology, the Food and Drug Administration, and NASA.

Most Marylanders work for private companies. Some private sector jobs are in high-skilled areas such as the manufacture of computer and electronic products and research in areas such as information technology, telecommunications, aerospace and defense industry, and medical or bioresearch laboratories. Other major private sector jobs are in food processing (soda, spices, seafood) and printing.

Agriculture also contributes to the economy of the state. More than one-third of Maryland's land is farmland. Chickens are the state's leading farm product. Other agricultural crops include nursery and greenhouse products, dairy products, corn, tomatoes, and soybeans.

With its many estuaries and rivers, Maryland has one of the longest waterfronts of any state—3,190 miles (5,134 km) of shoreline. For years. people living along the water have earned their living from fishing or harvesting blue crabs, clams, and oysters. The Chesapeake Bay is especially known for its seafood production. However, beginning around the mid-20th century the Bay showed a reduction in crab, clam, and oyster numbers. Scientists blame the decrease on pollutants and runoff from urban areas and from farms. Problems with the bay have prompted legislators to pass laws to protect the Chesapeake Bay watershed and reduce the runoff of pollutants.

## The People

Maryland is part of the East Coast urban corridor. With 594.8 people per

*Camden Yards, where the Baltimore Orioles play baseball, was built in a former warehouse district.*

square mile, the state is the seventh most densely populated in the nation.

According to the 2010 census, Maryland's population grew to 5,773,552 from 5,296,486 in 2000. The 9.0 percent increase ranked 15th among the 50 states.

U.S. Census data shows that Maryland is becoming more diverse in its population. Non-Hispanic whites made up 54.7 percent of the population in 2010, compared to 62.1 percent in 2000. In 2010 African Americans made up 29 percent of Maryland's population, Hispanics, 8.2%, and Asians, 5.5%.

# Some Famous Marylanders

Surveyor and astronomer Benjamin Banneker (1731–1806) of Ellicott City helped survey the District of Columbia, the capital of the United States.

Frederick-born Francis Scott Key (1780–1843) wrote the U.S. National Anthem, the "Star-Spangled Banner," after watching the battle of Fort McHenry in Baltimore during the War of 1812.

Born on the Eastern Shore of Maryland, activist and author Frederick Douglass (1818–1895) spoke out against slavery in the United States and Europe. After the Civil War he fought for the rights of African Americans and women.

Born a slave in Maryland's Dorchester County, Harriet Tubman (1819?–1913) was 30 years old when she escaped to freedom in Pennsylvania. She returned south many more times, eventually helping more than 300 slaves escape to freedom via the Underground Railroad.

Born in Anne Arundel County, financier and philanthropist Johns Hopkins (1795–1873) was the founder of Maryland's Johns Hopkins University in Baltimore. He also provided funding to establish a free hospital in the city, Johns Hopkins Hospital.

Baltimore-born civil rights activist Lillie Carroll Jackson (1889–1975) headed the city's National Association for the Advancement of Colored People (NAACP) for 35 years. Thurgood Marshall (1908–1993) of Baltimore was the first African-American appointed a justice of the United States Supreme Court.

Author and ecologist Rachel Carson (1907–1964) lived most of her life in Maryland. Her book *Silent Spring*, published in 1962, challenged the scientific community to consider the effect of chemicals and pesticides such as DDT on the environment.

Born in Baltimore, Maryland, U.S. Senator Barbara Mikulski (b. 1936), was elected to office in November 1986, becoming the 16th woman to serve in the Senate. Another politician born in Baltimore is House Minority Leader Nancy Pelosi (b. 1940), who is the first woman to serve as Speaker of the House.

# Major Cities

According to the U.S. Census bureau, more than 80 percent of Marylanders live in urban areas. (An urban area is defined as a region with more than 1,000 people per square mile.)

Founded in 1729, **Baltimore City** (620,961) is Maryland's most populous city. It is a major port of the eastern United States, handling imports such as automobiles, containers, and wood pulp. Exports include coal, corn, soybeans, petroleum and fuel oils. Major attractions of the city include its Inner Harbor area, which features the National Aquarium and the Maryland Science Center. Near the harbor are Fort McHenry National Monument and Historic Shrine and sports stadiums for the Baltimore Orioles baseball team and the Ravens football team.

Maryland's second most populous city, **Frederick** (65,239) is located about 45 miles north of Washington, D.C., at the intersection of two major interstates. Founded in 1745 by German settlers, the city serves as the county seat.

*Snow covered cemetery at the shrine of Saint Elizabeth Ann Seton in Emmitsburg. Seton (1774–1821) was the first American-born person to be canonized as a saint by the Roman Catholic Church.*

Other major urban areas in the D.C. metropolitan area are **Rockville** (61,209) and **Gaithersburg** (65,690). Gaithersburg is one of the fastest-growing cities in the United States.

Located on the Western Shore of Maryland, on the Chesapeake Bay and at the mouth of the Severn River, **Annapolis** is the state capital of Maryland and county seat of Anne Arundel County. Named in 1702 for Queen Anne of Great Britain and Ireland, the seaport city is also home to the U.S. Naval Academy.

# Further Reading

Cunningham, Kevin. *The Maryland Colony*. New York: Scholastic, 2011.

Jones, Rebecca C. *Captain John Smith's Big and Beautiful Bay*. Atglen, Pa.: Schiffer Publishing, 2011.

Otfinoski, Steven. *Maryland*. New York: Cavendish Square Publishing, 2014.

# Internet Resources

**http://www.mdkidspage.org/**

The office of Maryland's Secretary of State provides information on Maryland history, geography, and government.

**http://msa.maryland.gov/msa/mdmanual/01glance/html/mdglance.html**

More than 75 different topics on Maryland, provided by the state archives.

**http://www.visitmaryland.org/Pages/MarylandHome.aspx**

Official site of the Maryland Office of Tourism.

 # Text-Dependent Questions

1. Which major river runs along the southern border of Maryland?
2. What two key battles took place in Maryland during the Civil War?
3. How has immigration affected Maryland's population?

 # Research Project

When John Smith explored the Chesapeake Bay in the early 1600s he charted maps and documented what he saw. Using the Internet or your school library, find out more about what he discovered. Write a one-page report.

# Index

Numbers in **bold italics** refer to captions.

# Series Glossary of Key Terms

**bicameral**—having two legislative chambers (for example, a senate and a house of representatives).

**cede**—to yield or give up land, usually through a treaty or other formal agreement.

**census**—an official population count.

**constitution**—a written document that embodies the rules of a government.

**delegation**—a group of persons chosen to represent others.

**elevation**—height above sea level.

**legislature**—a lawmaking body.

**precipitation**—rain and snow.

**term limit**—a legal restriction on how many consecutive terms an office holder may serve.